Farmyard Friends
HORSES

Maddie Gibbs

PowerKiDS press.

New York

Dedication: *For Ali, since horses always make me think of her*

Published in 2015 by The Rosen Publishing Group, Inc.
29 East 21st Street, New York, NY 10010

First Edition

Editor: Caitie McAneney
Book Design: Katelyn Heinle

Photo Credits: Cover, p. 1 Melanie Hoffman/Shutterstock.com; p. 5 Irina Mos/Shutterstock.com; p. 6 Dhoxax/Shutterstock.com; pp. 9, 24 (foal) Volodymyr Burdiak/Shutterstock.com; p. 10 Takacs Szabolcs/Shutterstock.com; pp. 13 kazenouta/Shutterstock.com; p. 14 smeola/Shutterstock.com; p. 17 Cheryl Ann Quigley/Shutterstock.com; p. 18 Conny Sjostrom/Getty Images; p. 21 Jim Noetzel/Shutterstock.com; p. 22 gorillaimages/Shutterstock.com; p. 24 (stable), (stall) Artazum and Iriana Shiyan/Shutterstock.com.

Library of Congress Cataloging-in-Publication Data

Gibbs, Maddie, author.
 Horses / Maddie Gibbs.
    pages cm. — (Farmyard friends)
 Includes index.
 ISBN 978-1-4994-0144-8 (pbk.)
 ISBN 978-1-4994-0145-5 (6 pack)
 ISBN 978-1-4994-0143-1 (library binding)
 1. Horses—Juvenile literature. 2. Domestic animals—Juvenile literature. I. Title.
 SF302.G536 2015
 636.1—dc23
                              2014025297

Manufactured in the United States of America

CPSIA Compliance Information: Batch #CW15PK: For Further Information contact Rosen Publishing, New York, New York at 1-800-237-9932

CONTENTS

Do you like horses?
Most horses live on farms.

Male horses are called stallions.
Females are called mares.

Foals are baby horses.
Young females are called fillies.
Young males are called colts.

Horses are measured in hands. One hand is 4 inches (10 cm).

Horses live in **stables**.
Each horse in the stable gets
its own **stall**.

There are many kinds of horses. Arabian horses are from the Middle East.

Thoroughbreds were first raised in England. They are fast runners!

In the past, horses did a lot of the work on farms.

Today, people raise horses
to race or to ride.

Riding a horse is fun! Have you ever ridden a horse?

WORDS TO KNOW

foal

stable

stall

INDEX

WEBSITES

Due to the changing nature of Internet links, PowerKids Press has developed an online list of websites related to the subject of this book. This site is updated regularly. Please use this link to access the list: www.powerkidslinks.com/fmyd/hors